AF265443

(www.E-Mediatebooks.com).

First edition: March 2022
ISBN: 978-0-9569989-7-2

Cover: Rose: © Can Stock Photo / aprilphoto
          Chrysalis: © Can Stock Photo / Undy

Published by E-Mediate Books Ltd (www.E-Mediatebooks.com).

Working with...

IN THEIR BEST INTEREST

by

Charlie Foote

About Charlie Foote:

Charlie has been interested in Servant-Leadership since he first discovered it late in the 20th century. He was quickly introduced to The Greenleaf Centre for Servant-Leadership UK which held its first conference on Servant-Leadership in 1999. Charlie was there and has attended most of their annual conferences since then, and has presented at several. He has been a board member of the Centre for many years.

In 2013 Charlie also introduced an annual northern Servant-Leadership conference in Leeds. He has organised and presented at that conference.

As well as having theoretical knowledge, Charlie has introduced the principles of Servant-Leadership into several organisations, including three businesses he founded.

Sometimes the principles did not become permanent and the initiative has ended in failure. However, there was always a good reason, and Charlie took away valuable lessons. One thing that became clear to him is that a strong philosophical background was needed to bolster attempts to introduce Servant-Leadership.

Charlie tended to flounder when the going got tough – when, for example, senior colleagues became more interested in their own personal motives rather than the guiding motives of the organisation. He intends this book to go some way towards remedying a shortage of clearly stated, practical principles.

In 2006 Charlie founded Work AnyWare Ltd with Justin Gallagher. Work AnyWare was built from the start on Servant-Leadership principles, guided by Charlie's hard earned experience. It still runs as a Servant-Leadership organisation, and that influence is acknowledged on their web site. As a very successful business it shows that a Servant-Leadership based organisation can compete very effectively in a market economy.

CONTENTS

FOREWORD

Servant-Leadership is a way of looking at leadership that is both simple in theory and difficult in practice – the difficulties being the emphasis on our own advancement and a focus on the leader as a hero issuing commands and accomplishing the impossible.

Luckily many people have seen the poverty of this mindset and the harm it does to individuals, including leaders themselves and to those they are leading.

Through the writings of leadership theorists much has been developed since Robert Greenleaf first put forward his ideas on Servant-Leadership in the 1960's, but there still remains a gap in terms of practical day-to-day applications and what we need to do to be Servant-Leaders.

Fortunately, we have a true Servant-Leader, Charlie Foote, who has developed and run organisations with a Servant-Leadership focus. His book offers us a very clear and heart-felt approach to Servant-Leadership through looking after each others' best interests.

As Robert Greenleaf puts it "our highest priority needs". (Note it's about our needs not our wants). Charlie takes us through some very practical steps and attitudes to help us to orientate ourselves to service, as a choice of course not as a must. He looks at the skills we need to develop, paying attention, listening, asking, observing and acting out of care and generosity towards others and towards ourselves. He further demonstrates the benefits that this brings both to individuals and to organisations.

Charlie also is clear that this is about leadership and requires discrimination and courage if we are to act in others' best interests and not just give in to requests that may harm individuals and those around them. Finally, he suggests a number of self-reflective questions to help us on our journeys towards Servant-Leadership.

This is a tremendous contribution towards a better way of leading and coming as it does from practical experience gives us hope and a sense that we can become the leaders we deserve to be, both for others, but also for ourselves.

My sincere and grateful thanks to Charlie for a wonderful book.

Ralph Lewis,
founder with John Noble of the Greenleaf Centre for Servant-Leadership UK.

ACKNOWLEDGEMENTS

This book is partly based on my working experience, but also very much based on the many wonderful conversations I have had with others over the years, with so many people, about leadership in general and Servant-Leadership in particular.

There are too many to list – but you know who you are! Thank you all so much.

A special thanks to Ralph Lewis who helped me to refine the crude ore of my initial draft into the polished product you see today, and who has graced the book with a generous foreword.

A special thanks also to my publisher, Hazel Wood, who had more faith in me than I had in myself and has been a joy to work with.

1   **INTRODUCTION**

This book is about serving people in their best interests, in the context of Servant-Leadership.

Servant-Leadership was first mooted by Robert Greenleaf in the 1970s. He wanted large organisations to be better run and his recipe for achieving this was to base leadership firmly on service. He suggested that leaders should serve others, and that the most effective service to others is serving them in their best interests.

Service arises from a motive of caring. Leaders serve people by helping and supporting them in their work roles and in their life generally.

In order to serve people in their best interests we need to know what their best interests are, where they are in their working lives now, and where they would like to be. This book helps us to identify those things.

Some people are concerned by the concept of serving and feel that it has a demeaning connotation. They hesitate a little at the word servant in the phrase Servant-Leadership. We can lay that to rest.

The key lies in two concepts; choice and power. A traditional servant, in the sense used in the series *Upstairs Downstairs*, has neither choice nor power. They do as they are told and may be disciplined if they don't. They serve, but are powerless. They serve, but have little choice.

Those leading in our serving organisations serve by choice and from a position of strength. They don't have to serve, but choose to. They offer service with power. Their choice is based on a fundamental desire to help their colleagues and to help their organisation.

Servant-leaders don't seek to amass personal power. They share what power they have. Sharing power is not giving it away. Servant-leaders always retain enough power to be able to serve others in their best interests.

The choice to serve is based on personal values. Serving people is a caring thing to do. It is quite possible that by simple caring everyone's best interests can be served. This really does work much of the time. But a sense of care alone may not be enough when the going gets tough.

Then it is very helpful to have Servant-Leadership as a considered philosophy to fall back on which can help us to get through a hard time without abandoning the concept of service.

Service can be offered in several directions, for example, to our clients, to our purpose, to our organisation, to our employees or to wider society as a whole. We need to find a balance between these conflicting demands.

We hear people say that "The customer comes first". Customers are, of course, highly important. Servant-Leadership accepts their ultimate importance. But Servant-Leadership believes we need to serve our colleagues first since it is those colleagues who will

serve the customers. Our focus is on customers via colleagues.
Robert Greenleaf wanted to achieve better organisations.

By serving colleague in an unconditional way, and demanding little
in return, we find that:

- we get better work
- we get more cooperation and natural coordination
- we get more done – we achieve more
- we encourage initiative and creativity – we achieve better.

Giving disinterested service is our prime motive, but we have clear
secondary motives of surviving and thriving. Serving colleagues
will help our organisation to flourish, now and in the future,
because our well-supported colleagues are inspired to do their
best work and make a real difference to the way the organisation
runs and succeeds.

Serving others is talked about here in the context of organisations.
Organisations provide jobs and work for people. Servant-
Leadership has a concept of work which fits with treating people in
a humane way.

There is a view, a relic from the past, that people don't want to
work and have to be coerced into doing it. In older times jobs
could be meaningless, boring, stultifying, frightening and so on,
and perhaps at one time that view made sense. Those days are
now gone in our western society and people want to work.

Servant-Leadership encourages work, helping people become the
best they can be. It promotes and encourages the idea of serving
others in their best interest for the good it will bring.

There are two broad ways of getting a good thing to happen:

- we can encourage people to want it
- we can encourage people to offer it

We can encourage people to want to be served by taking away any reasons why they might resist it. After all, surely everyone wants to be served in their best interests?

However, there are occasions for resistance which arise from two main causes; misconception and suspicion. Some people mistake caring for weakness and hence they reject it. Others, who are perhaps used to a tougher working environment, are suspicious – why are you helping me? What's the catch?

We can overcome the problems of misinformation and suspicion by discussion and education, by publishing a formal statement of culture, and, most importantly, by example from our leaders and our peers.

Our culture of making work attractive and meaningful, and our inclusive approach, will make it clear to people that we are all in this together and that by supporting each other unconditionally we can achieve great things.

We can encourage people to offer service to others by similar means, and, importantly, by serving them first. We can further encourage them by education and discussion, by building it onto our culture, by setting a clear example, and by the beneficial effects of peer pressure.

We can make sure all our colleagues feel it is OK to support others, that they have our blessing to do so, and that the time it may take is well spent.

We can make it easier by removing any blocks which get in the way of giving service. For example, we can discourage internal competition between colleagues.

Greenleaf exhorts us to service in their best interests. This is how to do it.

IN THEIR BEST INTERESTS

2   IN THEIR BEST INTERESTS

Serving people in their best interests is a way of helping them to do what they would do themselves if they knew how, and if they felt they had permission to do so.

People have a general desire to know what their abilities are and to use them productively.

Servant-Leadership supports others in achieving a meaningful and satisfying working life, a satisfaction which can spill over, with benefit, into their life outside work.

To give service we need to be aware of ourselves – of our interests as well as their interests – and to balance the two with wisdom and compassion.

Service in Servant-Leadership is given because it is the right thing to do, rather than for expecting immediate benefits for the organisation. However, spin-off benefits do occur and we are unashamed to accept and welcome them.

Serving takes nothing away from us and yet gives something to others.

To serve others in their best interests four things seem to be needed:

- **Skill**

  (knowing how to put service into practice)

- **Discrimination**

  (knowing what service to give)

- **A good heart**

  (caring about those served)

- **Generosity**

  (giving without asking anything in return)

Serving people in their best interests means offering and providing support on occasions and not offering practical help when such help isn't needed. We never stifle the instinct to help but never force it on others.

Caring – the Motive for Serving

Caring is the basis of serving.

- It is from a motive of care that we serve others at all.
- It is from a motive of care that we serve others in their best interests.
- It is from a motive of care that we find out what those best interests are.
- It is from a motive of care that we check afterwards how well we served. "Did we do the right thing in the right way?" "How could we do it better next time?"

Moral Compass

We need a moral and social compass when working in others' best interests. We need to have wisdom to identify and balance the interests of the various 'those served'.

Moral compass gives us the courage to take the right action, not just what is expedient or convenient, and helps us to avoid actions with potentially harmful consequences.

Servant-Leaders perhaps need to be more honourable and more wise than leaders who operate simple command and control.

For the individual or the organisation?

Helping people in their best interests can result from a natural desire to be helpful, or from a desire to bring benefits to the organisation.

We take both into account, but perhaps the balance in Servant-Leadership is tipped toward the individual.

Desire To Be Helpful

There is a natural human desire to be helpful. It suits our nature to be kind to others. We have a human instinct to help.

If an elderly person trips and falls in the street everybody nearby will rush to help and see if she or he is OK. People don't do this so that they will be liked, or approved of. They just want to help.

This natural desire to be helpful applies at work, just as much as in the rest of life. We make sure that the simple desire to help is not suppressed.

Benefit To The Organisation

Serving people in their best interests has a beneficial spin-off to the organisation.

Well-treated colleagues work better, are better motivated and more productive. They, in their turn, also serve others better, such as customers and patients.

Well-treated colleagues also adapt better to change. All organisations have to face changing circumstances. We live in a volatile world. We never know when our product or service might become redundant. We need to be aware of current trends and creative in or response to them.

Well-treated colleagues are more flexible and adaptable. They notice change, report it honestly, and respond creatively to it as part of a team with their colleagues.

And if hard times hit us, they help keep the organisation on track, keeping bad impacts to a minimum, and being prepared to share in bad fall out.

It can't be denied that self-interest is involved. But for us it isn't a high priority motive. It doesn't override other motives, and is certainly not at the forefront of our minds.

Communal and Individual Best Interests

We can serve people's best interests by treating everyone in the workplace well, and we can also serve each individual's best interest directly.

The communal best interest is about having the ideal working environment. If the atmosphere is good everyone benefits. A good working atmosphere is the context in which the personal best interests of individuals can be truly served.

Who decides what is in our colleague's best interests?

The person deciding on others best interests may be the person offering service or the person receiving the service.

If the person giving the serving is alone in deciding, there is a danger of our becoming paternalistic. If the person receiving the service is alone in deciding there is a danger of our becoming indulgent. Both have to be taken into account to come up with the right mix.

All people are different, and all are different from us. We have to adapt to these differences to serve colleagues in their best interests.

What if Interests Clash?

There are potential clashes of interest each time someone is served in their best interests. Serving a particular individual may clash with the good of the organisation, or may cause resentment among the other employees.

As a simple example, we can imagine giving the parent of a very sick child four weeks paid compassionate leave to look after the child.

In doing so the organisation's capacity to operate is slightly reduced. This may have to be compensated for in a paid way, perhaps by bringing in temporary staff or offering overtime to existing staff.

Is such a small expenditure of any real danger to the organisation?

What about the effect on the other employees?

Some might feel that they have missed out. A sense of fairness is important. In Servant-Leadership organisations, fairness relates to equality of concern rather than equality of action.
Everyone is treated with equal compassion, but everyone's problems are different.

In practice most colleagues will be happy to see that a colleague who is suffering is being helped by the organisation.

Fear of Being Helpful

Some managers and leaders worry about serving people in their best interests. They can be fearful of where it might lead.

For example, they might be afraid that they will appear weak and lose respect; that colleagues will become lazy or dismissive; that the organisation will lose its competitive edge, or that people will take advantage of kindness and put in as little effort as they can get away with.

Some even fear that being empathetic makes them somehow vulnerable.

We rarely see these things happening in practice. Such problems occasionally arise, but very rarely, and in the few cases where they do they are easily dealt with.

How do we know if it's In Their Best Interests?

Mostly there isn't much doubt, but if we aren't sure we can ask.

If we suspect that a colleague doesn't really know what their best interests are we may be tempted to decide for them. This can be dangerous because it may reflect our prejudices rather than their interests.

We may need to look at ourselves and ensure we are acting with a good heart. We can test ourselves in any particular situation by imagining it happening to us. What is our emotional reaction?

THE SERVANT-LEADER'S MINDSET

Leaders serving others in their best interests have a mindset of service. The concept of a mindset is important because it makes clear what our intention is without making it a hard and fast rule.

We intend to give great service to our colleagues, but accept that sometimes we fail. In some circumstances we can't do it. By calling it a mindset, the occasional failure doesn't invalidate our intention. There is no sense in which events can knock it out. A mindset allows us to be temporarily wrong.

Servant-Leaders have many mindsets.

They have important mindsets about getting sales and earnings, coping with a competitive environment, developing products to ensure future success, and so on.

In this book we are talking about people and the relevant mindset is about leading from the standpoint of service.

It can be summed up as: **Care, Serve, Lead.** In that order.

Care is used in the sense of being concerned about. Without concern we are not motivated to serve. Once we serve we develop the motivation to take a lead.

A typical leader in a traditional organisation does it the other way round. They start with an urge to lead. Leading in practice tells the leaders that they have to take people into account and support them to get the best result for the organisation. Giving support to people gradually persuades those leaders that people matter.

The Servant-Leader's mindset is one of *unconditional support.*

We use the word unconditional in that sense that we offer service *without conditions*. That is, we help you without expecting something in return.

 We are saying "We will support you", not, " We will support you only if ...".

There is another sense of the word meaning that you will be supported whatever you do – in other words *anything goes*, a sense that is not at all consistent with Servant-Leadership.

We make a distinction between the person as a human, and the person's behaviour.

We do not tolerate people doing things which are legally wrong, such as stealing the petty cash, or whose behaviour is unacceptable to us, such trying to turn us away from Servant-Leadership, or blatantly seeking personal power. We are firm in not accepting bad behaviours.

Nevertheless, we try to support the human being, to help them overcome their problems if we can. We are never vindictive, even in the face of bad behaviour, but nor are we indulgent.

Many people are already serving others in their best interests, and are probably not doing it from the basis of Servant-Leadership. Service in others best interest is by no means restricted to those who follow the principles of Servant-Leadership. But it is an integral part of Servant-Leadership and it is worth knowing how the different aspects of Servant-Leadership combine to form a consistent philosophy.

There is more on Servant-Leadership and its practical use in organisations in my book *"Working with Servant-Leadership"*.

SERVING THE COMMUNAL BEST INTEREST

3   SERVING THE COMMUNAL BEST INTEREST

The interests of everyone in an organisation are best served by offering a great working environment; one which meets people's physical, intellectual, emotional and social needs, in which people are treated with care, respect, consideration and kindness. And hopefully being a joyous place to work – it is hard to be happy if others are unhappy.

As Servant-Leaders we want to create the ideal working environment for our colleagues and we want to make sure it stays that way.

Creating the Ideal Working Environment

Creating the ideal working environment is a matter of being aware of what it can be, and then setting about achieving it.

In this chapter we help to clarify the ideal working environment, based on serving others.

We can summarise a good place to work in several features. It is a place where:

- people can feel safe and yet challenged
- people want to do good work and are not hindered

- people are trusted
- people are treated like human beings
- people have a say in what they're doing
- people can be dedicated but also have fun
- people's ideas are listened to
- people can feel they are doing something useful to the best of their ability.

Servant-Leadership attempts to achieve this and sees it as in everyone's best interests.

These welcome features are built around several aspects of the workplace.

The physical environment offers comfort, stimulation, a place where it is easy to interact with others, but a place where we can be alone when we need to concentrate or reflect.

The intellectual environment offers individual and shared purpose, and a chance to be creative and develop.

The emotional environment offers a place we can be recognised and appreciated, where we can feel needed, and where we can trust and be trusted.

The social environment offers community, mutual support, and a feeling that we are all are in it together.

Some people describe this as creating an atmosphere of shared consciousness.

Reason to Work and Motivation

We are running an organisation, so getting work done must be paramount. People love to work as long as they think it's worthwhile, and as long as they are treated as worthwhile people.

People do their best work if they are given a good working atmosphere, knowledge of what they are supposed to be doing in general terms, and the freedom and autonomy to do good work within that framework.

People like to have some say in how they do things. They want to do a good job and continue to develop in their role, and they want to know how their work contributes to a wider purpose, which is itself a moral purpose.

People want to exercise their independence, but also want the safety net of being able to fall back on the support of the wider community when things get tough.

We support our colleagues in their best interests by building a culture in which they can be motivated in these ways.

Everyone has shared responsibility and the opportunity to provide their own unique expertise.

RESPECT

We offer true respect for our fellow human beings, recognising, valuing and caring for them. Our organisations are built on respect for everyone.

Respect protects the dignity of others, even when problems arise. Respect is a foundation of service. Everyone wants to be respected and treated with respect.

RIGHTS

People in work have employment rights, and Servant- Leadership organisations respect them and extend them. Rights are important, but need to be more than just words.

EQUALNESS

We are all individuals and we are all different. We don't have equal skills and talents. But we are all treated with equal care and respect as human beings. Fairness promotes well-being as well as productivity.

We use the word "equalness" rather than "equality" since we strive to have equal impact on people, rather than trying to help them all in exactly the same way.

TRUST

A good working environment depends on trust. An environment of trust helps people feel secure and reduces workplace stress and anxiety.

Trust is mutual. The more we trust others the more they trust us in their turn.

Trust is needed if people are to be successfully asked to change their routines or take risks. Trust is needed to operate a no blame culture. Trust is needed so that all sides can own up to mistakes, and allow essential learning to happen.

People need to trust us that we are serving colleagues in their best interests, and not in our own disguised interests.

To get trust we need to treat truth as important. Truth is more than the absence of lies. Our intention should not be to deceive.

Leaders need to trust their colleague to feel safe in leaving the detailed implementation to them without supervision.

SUPPORTIVE ATTITUDES

Some attitudes are conducive to building a great working environment. Attitudes are part of the organisation's culture.

There are too many to enumerate fully, but attitudes of caring, kindness, generosity, empathy, flexibility, appreciation and recognition are all found in Servant-Leadership organisations.

If someone's behaviour is hard to understand, we still care for and support them, even if their actions are not welcome.

POWER

It's no longer fashionable to use organisational power to get things done. Our intelligent and motivated work forces respond to other stimuli.

Organisations benefit from keeping a low power distance and benefit from making decisions without the oppressive use of power, instead using persuasion and involvement.

It has been found that a large power distance in operating theatres, between the surgeon and the nurses, inhibits useful feedback, and makes operations more likely to have poor outcomes.

HOPE

Hope is important in life for health and well-being. A great working atmosphere includes a sense of moving forwards, both as an organisation and as individuals.

In that way we can have a justified expectation of better things to come, of positive outcomes.

FUN AT WORK

We can laugh, tell jokes, mess about and share stories without damaging our purpose, or the quality of the work we do.

In fact, our purpose is served better when people are able to have some fun at work.

We know each other better, build friendships and communicate better. We are more creative. We generate a buzz which increases effort, contribution and cooperation.

It has a positive effect on our colleagues' well-being and can contribute to good health.

Maintaining the Ideal Working Environment

There may be challenges to even the best working environment and we have to recognise them and deal with them.

Here are some examples:

- Taking our eye off the ball – in a period of rapid growth our focus may slip away from maintaining the ideal environment

- We allow our serving culture to drift – in a period of rapid growth there may be an influx of new colleagues and until they are fully on board they may dilute our serving culture

- We make a recruitment mistake – we may accidentally recruit a toxic individual who sets about changing our culture.

Leaders who are serving people in their best interests will work out their own ways of solving these problems. The key thing is to be able to recognise them at an early stage and nip them in the bud.

Of course in moments of excitement we may easily get carried away. No harm is done as long as we take stock after a while and bring things back on track.

THE POSITIVE MESSAGE

People love working in a supportive environment as exemplified by a serving culture based on Servant-Leadership.

Our peers will make great efforts to protect that culture.

We have to let them know that their voices are important and will be listened to, and followed through in practice.

Then everyone involved will take steps to protect and maintain our ideal working environment.

At the time of writing many people are working at home because of Covid. We believe that having a supportive community at work is very important that many people will revert to office working as soon as it is safe to do so.

Every working environment has its plus and minus points and hence every environment can be improved.

Improving the environment is a team effort so, as far as possible, everybody should be involved in the process in an open conversation.

SERVING INDIVIDUALS' BEST INTERESTS

4 SERVING THE INDIVIDUALS' BEST INTEREST

The best interests of individual colleagues are served with specific support, offered to them alone, at the moment of serving.

We do things in three broad areas while serving individuals in their best interests

- we need to notice if something is not quite right, and help individuals to return to their optimum working

- we need to support people in doing their great work and encourage and help them to do it even better

- we need to look for potential in the people we work with, outside their current role, and help bring it out by offering greater responsibility or technical challenge

All three purposes are served by the techniques described in this chapter.

Techniques for Serving in Their Best Interests

To help people and serve them in their best interest we need to pay attention to them, by listening, observing, and, if relevant, taking heed of the observations of third parties.

Some colleagues need appreciation, some need communication, some want practical help, some want a sympathetic ear, some want to be encouraged and some just want to be left alone.

We are not imposing service and support on anyone. We are simply offering the best help, support and encouragement we can.

Serving others in their best interests is organised around five basic processes:

- **Pay attention**
- **Ask**
- **Stand in their shoes (empathy)**
- **Have the conversation**
- **Look at ourselves**

The most vital process is paying attention - listening and observing, and asking if and when we want to know more.

To give helpful service we need to find out where they are right now, and where they are coming from. We do this by imagining ourselves standing in their shoes.

To go deeper into any problems which arise, and find helpful solutions, we need to have an open conversation with the person affected. To cope with all this we need to look at ourselves, to know where we are coming from.

PAY ATTENTION

To know what someone needs or wants, we need to pay genuine attention to them. Paying attention is also taking an interest.

The basics of paying attention are simple to say but surprisingly hard to do well. We may listen to people without hearing. We may observe people without seeing. Or we may let our own thoughts mask the message.

The very act of paying attention to colleagues develops our ability to pay attention. We need to practice.

We listen to spoken words, and read written words. We look for the meaning behind the words. We listen to hear rather than to solve. Our colleagues want us to listen *through* their words to get to the common feelings we share.

If a colleague wants to share feelings with us, we give them the gift of receiving their offering. They can tell their story only if someone is there to listen. Listening alone is good, but we must also care.

The opposite of caring is not ill-treatment, it is indifference. Listening to someone is a gift to them. Failure to listen, even with good intentions, may result in our taking the wrong steps forward.

We observe facial expressions, body language and interactions with their colleagues. Observation is objective and not through the prism of our prejudices or emotional states.

To truly respect our colleagues, the attention we give them is without judgement or evaluation.

ASK

Sometimes, despite listening and observation, we don't fully understand. We can learn more by admitting we don't know and asking. It is good to ask subtly as asking can easily slip into a power exercise where the question effectively forces the answer.

To avoid power play it's best to use open questions, allowing the other to give their personal answer. Sometimes people are not sure of their own answer. We can help them come to it, but our promptings should lead them in their direction, not in ours.

STAND IN THEIR SHOES

To pay the right attention to people we need to enter into their consciousness, we need to stand in their shoes. It will help us to understand and empathise with them and serve them in their best interests.

Sometimes what seems like a clear benefit to the person offering service doesn't seem that way to the recipient.

If we can imagine what it is like for others, where they are standing now, it will help us serve them better.

HAVE THE CONVERSATION

Most relationship problems in an organisation can be solved by having the right sort of conversation. Conversation is the most important way of establishing equality between participants.

"Have the conversation" in our context is more than just making gentle enquiries. It arises when a decision is needed, or a solution to a difficulty in our relationship with others, is needed.

The situation is rarely one sided. Both sides have to identify their shared goals, and make compromises. We need to meet people where they are mentally, not where we want them to be.

For example, a leader may be constantly interfering with a colleague's work. There is clearly a problem to be solved. The leader may have to give up an "I know best" attitude, and hence the desire to interfere. The colleague may have to work a little differently or be more upfront about what they are doing and why.

To be effective the conversation has to be an open conversation between equals characterised by:

- being friendly and unthreatening
- avoiding rank
- using open questions
- staying away from guilt and blame
- not starting from an entrenched position
- not prejudging any outcome.

An open conversation is honest and cooperative. It happens without prejudging or pushing for any particular outcome. It is a way to interact, learn, and understand.

In an open conversation it is best to avoid "why" questions and "you" statements which can often appear to be criticism, even if none is intended.

"Why" questions can be interpreted by the listener as "Why on earth did you do that?"

"You" statements can be thought to imply blame. For example, "You always seem to act before thinking".

People dislike being wrong. They also dislike refusing to do things. They dislike being forced to say "no". In our open conversations we should avoid forcing people into these uncomfortable positions. It tends to polarise conversations, and hardens whatever position they are in. They become less willing to cooperate for mutual benefit.

We can sum this up in the phrase, "You may disagree with me, but don't make me wrong".

LOOK AT OURSELVES

We all have biases, and we need to know what they are in order to prevent them from negatively affecting our work, and our work relationships.

How we see people depends on our state of mind, which often we are not aware of. If we are angry we see people one way; if we are calm we see them another way. Yet the person remains the same.

Are we self-interested? Are we annoyed and resentful? These things kill an open conversation.

If we are aware of our own interests, and also those of the colleague in question, we can balance both with wisdom and compassion. This stresses the importance of leaders looking after themselves.

BEING PRESENT

Sometimes it is in the best interests of others to do nothing.

This is not neglect. We are "present" but not interacting. It's a sort of active presence. The leader observes, but if those served don't need help and support right now, it isn't given.

Some describe this sort of presence as like a mother watching her child playing. She doesn't interfere, but she is there if something goes wrong. Of course, we don't adopt a parental attitude in Servant-Leadership, but this example helps explain the concept of active presence.

If a colleague is seen to be struggling or heading in a dangerous direction we step in to provide appropriate support. But if not, we do nothing.

Style of Serving

WITHOUT RANK

The best ideas and compromises arise when people feel free to say what they think and respond honestly to what others suggest. This works best if the conversation can be between equal human beings. If one side has more power, the other side may respond with deference, even if that is not asked for or expected. The person with the most rank may have to set the scene by declaring the conversation to be without rank.

Without rank we can avoid feelings of accusation and blame that are detrimental to producing a helpful outcome in the best interests of the person being served in the particular instance.

NON-PARTISAN STYLE

People can tell if we are acting honestly, in their best interests and can easily tell if we are acting in our own interests, but pretending it's for them.

We give help and support because they are fellow human beings, not because this will benefit us. Supporting needs to be genuine.

We serve others for its own sake – it is about them, not us.

Helping People Grow and Develop

One aspect of paying attention to people is noting their potential for creative personal development. We look out for exceptional abilities among colleagues, even in areas which might be new to them, and help them to develop and utilise those talents.

Everyone wants to Develop

We can encourage colleagues to attend training courses, learn a skill online, or to try new things – perhaps spending time in other work areas.

One method of doing this is to give each employee a training budget that they can spend on any course, with any delivery they like, no questions asked. Any new skill, learned with an open mind, will enhance job performance.

We mustn't fight for it to be relevant – we leave that to the person involved.

When a person wants to develop they may see their best option as moving out of our organisation. How should we react? If they are moving to a better opportunity we can encourage them to do so, with our blessing.

We don't want to trap people in our organisation, even by bonds of loyalty.

Serving and being served are self-reinforcing. The more we support others in their best interests the more likely they are to support us in return.

Our natural inclination is to help, and we also feel good about ourselves for doing so. We can recall the feelings we had when we were caring and helpful to others, and how they reacted. And we can remember how it felt when others were caring and supportive to us.

SOME PRACTICAL CONSIDERATIONS

5   SOME PRACTICAL CONSIDERATIONS

Once we have paid appropriate attention to colleagues, any action we take as leaders can be guided by common humanity.

As long as we truly aim to serve others in their best interests, whatever we do for them will be valuable and helpful.

The key is to do what is right – and we always try. However, sometimes we just don't get it right.

We are, after all, the usual bundle of human weaknesses trying to do the best we can. We can go wrong despite our good intentions.

In this chapter we offer a list of positive actions we might take. The point of the list is not to share what we all know already, but to make it clear that all these things are not just allowed, but encouraged.

If we are not thinking of doing these things we are inhibiting our leadership.

There is no reason, whether from conventional wisdom, management theory or whatever, to not act in these positive ways. If we find ourselves resisting them then we need to look at ourselves and our own reluctance. As leaders we not only can do these things, but we must when the need arises.

Even when we have established a need for action, we may not take it. Some of the common things which may hold us back are discussed in the next chapter.

THE SERVING PROCESS

In serving others, the server and the served interact – each trying to understand the other. The server mustn't assume they understand. We support our colleagues if they ask us to, or if we see they need help and support.

We have to refresh our skills each time we offer support.

LIST OF ACTIONS

Sometimes the best thing we can do is nothing. But other than that:

Remedial *Bringing back on course after a problem*	Offering moral support Having meaningful conversations Adjusting relationships Reallocating tasks Practical job support and advice Clarifying roles Offering a less demanding set of tasks Allocating alternative work they like better or are better suited to Offering a different role, without promotion, after appreciating that a person wants to try a completely new role, moving from, say, support to sales

Advancing *Encouraging better performance in the current role*	Offering active encouragement Planting new ideas Advanced job support and advice Give praise Recognise and acknowledge the good work being done Offering a more demanding set of tasks
Furthering *Developing talent into new areas*	Note special talents and try to use them Have a meaningful conversation about the future Encourage people to take on a bigger challenge Promote Offer a role with more leadership Change roles Promotion of role after noticing at special talent or experience, and helping the other to develop it Offering a role where they can be most effective
Outside work	Help people with their lives outside work. We can choose to take that into account. For example, giving time off or emergencies of compassionate reasons Practical help such as in-house pay-day loans The chance to work part-time or from home

None of this serving is possible without listening, watching, considering and caring.

When we are not in a leadership position we may still want to serve and support our colleagues. We can use some of the techniques in the table.

Where we may go wrong

We all make mistakes. We can learn from them. We need the courage to face our mistakes, to be accepting of the truth, and to stay humble... and all this while retaining enough self-confidence to carry on serving!

Here are some of the traps we can fall into.

Assuming everybody understands equality

Colleagues may respond unexpectedly. We may feel we are offering support with a clear feeling of equality, but the recipient may not see it that way.

They may give us unasked for deference – perhaps being unable to get away from automatically respecting our position in the hierarchy, or because we are older or more experienced.

IGNORING SIGNS

We may simply not notice that a colleague needs help and inadvertently neglect them. Often they will notice our neglect but say nothing.

Even if not intended harmfully, neglect may affect people's feelings of self-worth.

There is a clear difference between leaving someone alone, under a watchful eye, and not paying enough attention.

NO FOLLOW-UP

We may have good intentions but not show it. We don't mean to, but we do. We might not follow through, or delay to the point where action is seen as too late.

In doing so we fail to serve others in their best interests. We may be too shy to get involved, or feel we have no right to, despite the fact that we have picked up a signal of a problem.

Not acting as a result of timidity is no help. Acting in others best interests is a minor act of bravery for some.

In general failure to act means we have placed focus on our own interests, not on the interest of the person being served.

Having good intentions is not the same as doing something.

WITHHOLDING

Sometimes we find ourselves withholding help because we believe that others will step in and provide the support. Or we may withhold from baser reasons. Perhaps because we blame the other for the situation they find themselves in "It's your own fault", or get annoyed because help wasn't appreciated last time "I'm not wasting my time talking to you".

PATERNALISM

Paternalism is "telling people what is best for them". It is a claim that a person affected will be better off from our advice, even though their consent hasn't been asked for.

The good side of paternalism is that it comes out of a feeling of benevolence towards the other – we want to do what is best for them. At its root it is a caring impulse.

The not-so-good side is that it can have an unhealthy effect on autonomy and liberty of the person on the receiving end. It doesn't allow people to be who they are, to develop their talents, to overcome obstacles and to grow and develop.

In practice, nobody benefits from paternalism, including the people who are being paternalistic.

SELF-CONGRATULATIONS

Servant-Leadership promotes providing service to people for its own sake, not for selfish benefit.

Servant-Leadership discourages leaders to boast about their enlightened approaches, saying such things as "Didn't I do well" or "Aren't they grateful". This sort of self congratulation tends to reinforce the image of the "boss" as an irreplaceable figure.

Servant-Leadership, with its focus on stewardship, encourages us to play down the concept of "irreplaceable figures" so that the business can survive and thrive without them.

CRITICISING

Criticising people or telling people they are wrong, discourages them and reduces motivation. It isn't in their best interests, but nor is letting errors go unremarked.

A better approach is to help others to see, as part of an open conversation, how a different approach would have been more beneficial. Each side can learn without feeling they have been put down.

An aspect of criticism which needs some attention is the use of "why" questions. "Why" questions can be very useful in other contexts, for example, when deciding on strategy or tactics in a group context.

However, when things are not going well "why" questions are often seen by the recipient as critical of them. In their own minds they translate the "why" question into "How could you do something as silly as that."

Instead we rephrase the intervention with something more open-ended, allowing the other to state their understanding without starting from a point of feeling criticised. Phrasing can be something like "I'm not sure what is happening here – can you fill me in?" might work.

BLAMING

A "no blame" culture at work is a good support to productive work. Being blamed can have consequences, it can make us less adventurous and more risk averse. We may not do our best work for fear of being blamed'.

When we talk about a no blame culture we are not talking about a no responsibility culture

When we do something we are responsible for it. If it goes wrong, even in a no blame culture, we remain responsible.

However, we accept that we've made a mistake. We can apologise to the person affected if that makes sense and, more importantly, we can learn from it and share our learning with others.

We can take responsibility without being blamed.

JUDGING

We don't judge people, we serve them.

We don't decide if they are good or bad people. We look for the good in them. All behaviour is human behaviour – nothing is "non-compliant".

People who feel judged as human beings don't easily accept help, and may not even engage in a supportive conversation. It becomes hard for us to work in their best interests.

We do need to judge performance, but not human value.

INTERFERING

"Why do we interfere?".

Do we see it as being helpful to the person served?
– "I'm doing it for you".

Do we see it as helping our organisation?
– "I'm doing it for us".

Or is it built in to our personality
– "I'm doing it for me".

To be persistently interfering with someone's work is in neither's interest. Do we think that their work is such that they have to be kept on course by constant corrections? Or is it that it's our personality to interfere?

DEMANDING

Using a demanding tone is not good for co-operation. It can make colleagues feel that they personally have been given a task and will be blamed if it goes wrong. They may over focus on this task rather than caring about what the team is trying to achieve and this can mitigate against team effort.

All jobs are demanding on occasions, but people don't need to be driven like cattle to respond to these demands. It can be tempting to revert to command and control – simply telling the other what to do, rather than ask and encourage.

A small amount of pressure can occasionally inspire our colleagues to rise to a challenge, although conscientious colleagues are likely to be self-motivated enough to rise to the challenge anyhow, without pressure.

HECTORING

Constantly reminding someone that they haven't completed their work, or even worse, that they are not a successful employee gives a very strong message "We do not trust you".

Failing to trust colleagues is very detrimental to their best interests and may make a job stressful to the point that people need time off work to recover.

CLAIMING WE KNOW BEST

While attempting to serve people in their best interests we might confuse our interests with theirs or make the wrong moves.

Some people, who firmly believe they are right, often find it hard to watch someone do things in a different way, and may (from a fair motive) get in the way and insist that the task is done their way.

BEING WRONG

We might, for example, over-delegate. We allocate a task to someone, and they find it too difficult. The intention was to serve their best interests by challenging them in a helpful way. But we got it wrong.

HARASSING

(including intimidation, bullying, prejudice, etc)

Bullying and harassment are very serious concerns. They are very clearly in no-one's best interests.

These sorts of horrible behaviours are intended to undermine, humiliate, denigrate, injure or degrade the recipient.

They are an absolute anathema in any Servant-Leadership organisation. A zero tolerance policy is essential.

If there are victims, caring support for them, from the organisation, is paramount.

OVERCOMING THESE PROBLEMS

How can we avoid actions which inhibit our ability to serve others in their best interests?

We need to:

- be aware of what we are doing

- have appropriate conversations leading to compromise and future intentions

- stop our unhelpful behaviour.

BEING AWARE

We need to ask ourselves a number of questions:

"Is this really in their best interests?"

"How am I contributing to this difficulty?"

"Are my actions making things worse?

"Why am I doing this?" – are my motives straightforward and honest.

DISCUSS AND COMPROMISE

We need to raise the issue with the colleague concerned in an open conversation. We need to discuss a way forward, find a compromise and agree and accept that we will have to change, and acknowledge our agreement. And then commit ourselves to change.

STOP

Then we have to just stop.

SIGNS OF SUCCESS

6   SIGNS OF SUCCESS

How can we tell we have been successful at serving people in their best interests?

We need evidence in two aspects:

- How do I know I've managed it personally?
- What effect does it have on my organisation if we all do it?

Evidence of Personal Success

We may know we've succeeded if people say so, which is always nice to hear.

They may show it in their faces, with a certain joy or satisfaction shining through. We mostly can't disguise the emotions which show in our faces.

Over time we can see people change. Serving people in their best interest creates a supportive atmosphere in which they can safely change, on their own, in their own time.

Servant- Leadership doesn't aim to induce change, but it happens. Being cared for can make greedy people generous, aggressive people amenable and fixed people flexible.

People well-served credit themselves with success.

If we truly serve someone in their best interests they often feel they have done it themselves, either individually, or in their team.

That is the outcome we want to achieve. Their attitude adds to people's pride, self-esteem, enthusiasm and creativity. Success is great so let's have more of it. We can regularly ask ourselves:

"Did I handle this well?"

"How, with the benefit of hindsight, would I do it differently?"

Serving others in their best interests works for them and it works for us. It works for the people who, through service, have a happier, more meaningful and satisfying life.

And it feels like the right thing to be doing.

Evidence of Organisational Success

When leaders serve their colleagues in their best interests it has a beneficial effect on the whole organisation. It becomes more effective and efficient; more creative and resilient.

The evidence of success can be seen by these factors:

- The working environment improves to become more vibrant and creative, with colleagues showing a real desire to meet the organisations purpose

- Colleagues increasingly cooperating and supporting each other in improving the products and services on offer, and how they are delivered to clients

- Colleagues growing and developing in their working lives, with a growing conviction that they are doing something with a real purpose and value

- Colleagues, being served well themselves, give great service to their client base

- Colleagues show enthusiasm for helping the local community – for example, a programmer may help to set up a code club at a local school

- The organisation reports better financial results
- The organisation retains good people, and attracts good recruits, thus ensuring the long term viability of the organisation.

With success comes the desire to do more. We need to assess honestly how well we have done, to acknowledge where we have been successful, and hence build on our desire to serve more and serve better.

HELPING YOURSELF TO SERVE

7   HELPING YOURSELF TO SERVE

Introduction – This is about You

This chapter is a self-help chapter. Helping you to practice "in their best interests" in your working life.

In this chapter the focus is on you, the reader, and how you can help yourself to be better at serving *in their best interests* and to feel more at home with it.

We certainly don't know all the answers, but we do know that it is always good to try. Every bit of *in their best interests* effort has a benefit – every attempt helps.

Levels of In Their Best Interests

There are no absolute levels of *in their best interests*, but here is our notional list, simply for the purposes of discussion:

Base level   – Becoming aware of the concept

Middle level   – Find out more about it – reading this book
                for example
        – Noticing that your behaviour affects others
        – Deciding to do something about serving others

Practice level – Trying it out and seeing the results, and then doing more
– Getting better at it – enhancing lives of colleagues
– Integrating it into your personality and leadership style

The point of raising these levels is to show that by serving at any of these levels a leader will be helping people – any service in the interest of others is better than none.

You don't have to be a star – you just have to care. Every effort you make, at any level, will make a difference to someone somewhere.

- *At what level of in their best interests am I operating at now?*
- *What steps can I take to increase my level?*

Success and Failure

There is no failure in giving this service in the best interest of others, apart from simply not trying. Any attempt to offer service is a step forward. Success follows honest effort. We think of serving others in their best interest as a mindset as described in an earlier chapter.

Be wary of setting specific success goals – it can be counterproductive. If you set yourself, say, a weekly "helping" target you are introducing the chance to fail in your own eyes and you may be tempted to force unwanted service on colleagues just to meet your own target.

Far better to have an attitude of *in their best interests* and express this by paying attention, caring and stepping in to give support when circumstances are right.

Servant-Leaders don't go actively looking for the opportunity to serve others, they do it as the need arises.

Developing your Practice of Serving in Other's Best Interests

We can compare learning to practice *in their best interests* with learning to drive a car. Some people have more natural aptitude than others, but eventually we all pass the test. To become a driver you have to learn the basic skills. After you pass the test you really start to learn how to drive by doing it.

The first long drive a person takes will leave a new driver exhausted because they have to focus their attention the whole time.

Once they are experienced they can let their attention drop for much of the journey, knowing that it will instantly return when the need arises.

Serving people *in their best interests* is like that. Once you are accustomed to it you are not constantly scanning your colleagues to see if they need help.

You are doing your day job and focusing on the problems you have to solve. But when you pick up a human signal you rapidly switch focus into serving the people involved.

Honing Your People Skills

Before you start driving a car you have to practice starting the car, steering, letting in the clutch, changing gear etc. In their best interests needs key skills to be developed too.

These have been discussed earlier in the book – paying attention, watching, listening and so on, These skills can be studied and learned. There's no substitute for practice.

No one starts off as an expert in anything. Everyone has to practice to get better. Serving people as a deliberate activity can seem artificial at first. But without practice it will never become ingrained and natural.

- *Do I feel that it is right to use softer human skills in leading my unit?*
- *Have I investigated or studied people skills such as listening, empathising?*
- *Have I tried to use these skills in my leadership role? How did it go?*
- *Have I created opportunities to practice these skills?*

It is important that you feel *allowed* to serve others in their best interests. People sometimes feel that they are not allowed to behave certain ways because it is against the culture of leadership, or against conventional wisdom. Sometimes people think caring is weakness or even anti-business, or that it is important "not to get involved".

Honest caring is always good. You are allowed to care.

- *Do I give myself permission to care for people?*

A Simple In Their Best Interests Mantra

It might be useful to have a mantra during the early stages of practicing serving others *in their best interests* – similar to the one for learning driving – Mirror-Signal-Manoeuvre.

One possibility might be Engage-Observe-Act.

- *Can I devise a mantra to help me while I am developing my* In Their Best Interests *skills?*

Each time you interact with a person, even if the interaction is simply passing each other in the kitchen, you can say to yourself your equivalent of the driving mantra. What do I notice? Are they content, self-involved, or whatever. Do I feel they need any sort of support? If unsure, ask a question. You will know them and hence know whether to try a direct or a roundabout approach - whatever works for them.

As your practice develops you will naturally forget the mantra as you will have internalised it,

Caring for People

- *Do I care about the people I work with? If not, am I in the wrong job? Or are they?*

- *How do I show my care in practice?*

- *How well do I balance care for myself with care for others? Servant-Leadership is neither self sacrifice or self interest – its a balance between the two.*

- *Am I courageous enough in doing what is right, not just what is convenient or expedient?*

Limits to Serving

Every colleague will have a concept of their own best interests. You can only serve those best interests which lie within the boundaries of your organisation's culture.

For example, a colleague may request a company car, in what he sees as his best interests. Your organisation does not offer them. In that case you will choose not serve him in what he sees as his best interest.

Colleagues best interests must fit in with the organisation's best interests. Your Servant-Leadership culture is important. You cannot allow individuals to abuse it.

- *Do I have clear boundaries beyond which I will not serve people, even if they claim it is in their best interest?*

Not Living up to Service in others best interest

- *Am I able to care for others and serve them in their best interests when I am under pressure?*

In the heat of the moment we may lose our people-focus. We all need to stop our own personal feelings getting in the way of service - even though service itself arises as a result of the emotion of caring. If we focus too much on ourselves and our problems we lose the focus on others.

Could I have done better?

We can always do better, although it's not helpful to beat ourselves up about it. For example, we may, in one instance, have over-focussed on the problem at the expense of the people. Or we may realise that we have accidentally ignored a particularly quiet member of the team.

You can spot situations you might have handled differently by the reaction of the people around you, by what they tell you, or just by the look on their faces.

- *Do I reflect on instances where I have served others to see how I might have done things better?*

- *Do I reflect on instances where I failed to offer support, but perhaps should have?*

- *Do I learn from cases where I slipped up?*

Most roles with a people-skills content ask that you reflect on how it went, and learn from each encounter. This is the way to get better and gain wisdom. Sometimes talking through your actions with a supportive colleague can add insight.

- *Do I use a colleague as a sounding board to work through problems?*

Roundup Session

Serving others in their best interest is best done by keeping your eyes open and watching for signs rather than seeing it as a continuous, active process. But every so often it's a good idea to set aside a little time to think about all the people you are leading.

You can, in your own mind, consider each of them in turn to check that they are OK and contented in their work. You can think where they are and what they might need.

If you have evidence or a gut feeling that someone needs help you can start the process. If they are fine, do nothing this time. If in doubt you can always talk to them.

Intuition

- *Do I take note of my intuitions about people?*

- *Do I consciously check that my intuitions reflect reality?*

Intuition, or gut feeling, is an important part of any human skill, and that is certainly true of *in their best interests.*

We have to be able to listen to our gut feelings, never denying them, but never relying on them uncritically. They need to be consciously checked against reality.

We all need to listen to what our intuition is telling us in *this situation,* now.

It is dangerous to recall earlier gut feelings. And any gut feeling needs to be disinterested, that is, not about what you want out of it. If you suspect it isn't disinterested, ignore it.

Integrating Service with Leadership

This book is principally about the *service* aspect of Servant-Leadership. But we mustn't forget the *leadership* aspect if we want to build well-rounded servant-leaders. The founding document of Servant-Leadership was entitled "The Servant as Leader". In other words it's about being a leader, using service as a basis.

Problem and People Skills

Leaders need to deliver on what they are there for. They can do this by focussing on the problems/tasks at hand, or by focussing on the people and human factors.

All leaders have to balance, in their leading role, these problem skills and people skills.

- *Does my personality lead me to focus more on problems than people, or more on people than problems?*

- *Have I achieved the right balance between problem focus and people focus?*

- *Have I honed my problem skills by reading, study, training courses, guided practice?*

- *Have I honed my people skills by reading, study, training courses, guided practice?*

- *Do I need to do more?*

Most leaders and managers have been taught and/or learned problem skills. Fewer have been taught or learned people skills.

In Servant-Leadership we see the need to develop skills of listening, trusting, supporting, empathy and offering people a feeling of purpose. Such skills are often thought of as intuitive, but they can nevertheless be developed by study and practice.

If, as a leader, you want to increase output you can use problem-type techniques – targets, incentives, discipline, or you can use people-type techniques – encouragement, care and support. Or a sensible balance of both.

It's hard to offer upfront advice on achieving balance because every situation is different. But if in doubt, Servant-Leadership favours tipping the balance slightly in favour of people skills.

This is not an attempt to overvalue people skills, but to restore the balance between people and problem skills, and to counter the overemphasis on problem skills that conventional organisations have built up over the decades.

Above the fray – the Third Leadership Skill Set

There is a third skill set needed, one which enables you to use the other skill sets effectively, and to combine them seamlessly for the best result. We can call this *wisdom*.

Wisdom depends on you, your personality and your experiences. And it includes traits such as being honourabe, being inspiring, and offering unconditional support.

You need wisdom to balance the use of the various skills you have available.

Achieving Balance

There is no "mathematical" way of deciding balance between the use of different skill sets – it's down to you, your values, your talents, in the situation you are in, with the colleagues you have, now.

- *Do I effectively balance the needs of the problem with the needs of the people/colleagues?*

- *Do my leading and serving skills work together seamlessly as effectively?*

- *What is my style for getting better performance?*

- *Am I problem-focussed tending to use methods such as targets, incentives, punishments?*

- *Am I people-focussed tending to use methods such as trusting, serving, support, helping?*

- *Am I able to combine both effectively?*

You can't serve others if you yourself are not in a good place. Serving others is helped by serving yourself.

- *Do I look after myself carefully enough?*

- *Can I effectively balance my interests with those of the ones I serve?*

Attempting a rational analysis to achieve is often too slow for real life. You may have to act quickly so that the time for helpful action doesn't slip away

You cannot accept decisions outside the envelope of the organisation's culture. You keep to yourself the power to veto. But vetoing it must be genuine, not just a way of getting what you selfishly want.

We find that in practice, in organisations based on Servant-Leadership, the overruling of colleagues in this way is very rare indeed.

Conclusion

Effective Servant-Leaders we need problem skills and person skills, and the wisdom to balance their use. They need to make effective use of teams, pointing them in the right direction, and serving and supporting them in achieving great things for the organisation.

Servant-Leaders need to trust people and earn their trust.
The author would like you to be a Servant-Leader, and to influence your organisation towards using Servant-Leadership principles.

We do so because we believe it results in better organisation.
Smarter, inclusive, sustainable.

These are the final questions to ask yourself.

- *Do I want to become a Servant-Leader?*

- *Do I want my organisation to be run on Servant-Leadership lines?*

FURTHER READING

Charlie Foote, *Working with Servant-Leadership*, E-Meditate Books Ltd, 2020

Ralph Lewis and John Noble, *Servant-Leadership – Bringing the Spirit of Work to Work*, Management Books 2000 Ltd., 2008

James Autry, *Love and Profit – The Art of Caring Leadership*, Avon Books, 1991

Kent M Keith, *The Case for Servant-Leadership,* The Greenleaf Center, 2015

There are also several organisations around the world dedicated to Servant-Leadership.